I0428827

U.S. ENVIRONMENTAL PROTECTION AGENCY

OFFICE OF INSPECTOR GENERAL

American Recovery and Reinvestment Act Site Visit of Wastewater Treatment Plant Improvements Project, City of Nappanee, Indiana

Report No. 12-R-0789   September 12, 2012

Scan this mobile code
to learn more about
the EPA OIG.

Report Contributors: Jean Bloom
                                                       Shannon Schofield
                                                       John P. Flynn
                                                       John Burns

Abbreviations

CFR	Code of Federal Regulations
EPA	U.S. Environmental Protection Agency
IFA	Indiana Finance Authority
OIG	Office of Inspector General

Cover photo: Digester building and drying shed at Nappanee, Indiana,
                    Wastewater Treatment Improvements Plant. (EPA OIG photo)

Hotline

To report fraud, waste, or abuse, contact us through one of the following methods:

e-mail: OIG_Hotline@epa.gov   **write:** EPA Inspector General Hotline
phone: 1-888-546-8740   1200 Pennsylvania Avenue NW
fax: 202-566-2599   Mailcode 2431T
online: http://www.epa.gov/oig/hotline.htm Washington, DC 20460

At a Glance

Why We Did This Review

The U.S. Environmental Protection Agency, Office of Inspector General, conducts site visits of American Recovery and Reinvestment Act of 2009 (Recovery Act) clean water and drinking water projects. The purpose of our visit was to address a hotline complaint involving compliance with the Recovery Act's Buy American requirements. The city received a $4,875,000 loan from the Indiana Finance Authority (IFA) under the Indiana Wastewater State Revolving Fund Loan Program. The loan included $1,769,000 in Recovery Act funds. The city used these funds to rehabilitate and improve its wastewater treatment plant.

This report addresses the following EPA Goal or Cross-Cutting Strategy:

• *Protecting America's waters*

For further information, contact our Office of Congressional and Public Affairs at (202) 566-2391.

The full report is at:
www.epa.gov/oig/reports/2012/
20120912-12-R-0789.pdf

American Recovery and Reinvestment Act Site Visit of Wastewater Treatment Plant Improvements Project, City of Nappanee, Indiana

What We Found

In September 2010 and May 2011, we visited the Wastewater Treatment Plant Improvements Project in the City of Nappanee, Indiana. As part of our site visit, we toured the project, visually inspected equipment and materials, interviewed IFA and city officials and their employees, reviewed manufacturers' substantial transformation supporting documentation, and reviewed documentation related to Buy American requirements.

We noted in our draft report 7 of 32 instances where the city could not demonstrate compliance with Buy American requirements as set out in Section 1605 of the Recovery Act. In response, the city provided documentation and agreed to take corrective actions to replace two items with products that meet the Buy American requirements. We agree that six of the seven items now comply with the requirements. For the one remaining item, the city could not demonstrate that it was manufactured in the United States, as required by the Recovery Act. As a result, the project is not eligible for the $1,769,000 of Recovery Act funds authorized by the state unless the U.S. Environmental Protection Agency exercises a regulatory option.

Recommendations and Planned Agency Corrective Actions

We recommend that Region 5 employ the procedures set out in Title 2 of the Code of Federal Regulations (CFR) to ensure compliance with the Buy American requirements. If the region decides to retain the foreign manufactured goods in the Nappanee project under 2 CFR §176.130 (c)(3), the region should either "reduce the amount of the award by the cost of the steel, iron, or manufactured goods that are used in the project or ... take enforcement or termination action in accordance with the agency's grants management regulations." We also recommend that the region require IFA to verify the city's corrective actions taken and ensure the replaced items meet the Buy American requirements.

Neither the region nor the city agreed with our conclusion that the documentation was not sufficient to support Buy American compliance. The Agency agreed with our recommendation to verify the city's corrective actions, and indicated the Agency visited the project and verified the agreed-to removal and replacement of items.

UNITED STATES ENVIRONMENTAL PROTECTION AGENCY
WASHINGTON, D.C. 20460

September 12, 2012

<u>MEMORANDUM</u>

SUBJECT: American Recovery and Reinvestment Act Site Visit of
Wastewater Treatment Plant Improvements Project,
City of Nappanee, Indiana
Report No. 12-R-0789

FROM: Arthur A. Elkins, Jr.

TO: Susan Hedman
Regional Administrator, Region 5

This is our report on the subject site visit conducted by the Office of Inspector General of the U.S. Environmental Protection Agency (EPA). This report contains findings that describe the problems the OIG has identified and corrective actions the OIG recommends. This report represents the opinion of the OIG and does not necessarily represent the final EPA position. Final determinations on matters in this report will be made by EPA managers in accordance with established audit resolution procedures.

We performed this site visit as part of our responsibility under the American Recovery and Reinvestment Act of 2009 (Recovery Act). The purpose of our site visit was to determine the city's compliance with Buy American requirements under Section 1605 of the Recovery Act pertaining to the Clean Water State Revolving Fund program. The Indiana Finance Authority approved the city's project. The city received a $4,875,000 loan, including $1,769,000 in Recovery Act funds.

Action Required

In accordance with EPA Manual 2750, Chapter 3, you are required to provide us your proposed management decision for resolution of the findings contained in this reported before any formal resolution can be completed with the recipient. Your proposed decision is due in 120 days, or on January 10, 2013. To expedite the resolution process, please e-mail an electronic version of your proposed management decision to adachi.robert@epa.gov.

Your response will be posted on the OIG's public website, along with our memorandum commenting on your response. Your response should be provided as an Adobe PDF file that complies with the accessibility requirements of Section 508 of the Rehabilitation Act of 1973, as amended. The final response should not contain data that you do not want to be released to the public; if your response contains such data, you should identify the data for redaction or removal. We have no objection to the further release of this report to the public. This report will be available at http://www.epa.gov/oig.

If you or your staff have any questions regarding this report, please contact Melissa Heist, Assistant Inspector General for Audit, at (202) 566-0899 or heist.melissa@epa.gov; or Robert Adachi, Product Line Director, at (415) 947-4537 or adachi.robert@epa.gov

American Recovery and Reinvestment Act
Site Visit of Wastewater Treatment Plant
Improvements Project, City of Nappanee, Indiana

12-R-0789

Table of Contents

Appendices

Purpose

The purpose of the site visit was to determine whether the City of Nappanee, Indiana, complied with Buy American requirements under Section 1605 of the American Recovery and Reinvestment Act of 2009 (Recovery Act), Public Law 111-5, pertaining to the Wastewater Treatment Plant Improvements Project jointly funded by the Recovery Act and the Indiana Wastewater State Revolving Fund Loan Program. We selected the project for review based upon a hotline complaint.

Background

In July 2009, the U.S. Environmental Protection Agency (EPA) awarded over $94 million of Recovery Act funds to the State of Indiana to capitalize its revolving loan fund, which provides financing for construction of wastewater treatment facilities and other authorized uses. In addition to the regulatory requirements at Title 40 Code of Federal Regulations (CFR) Chapter 1, Subchapter B, the assistance award was subject to Grants and Agreements; Award Terms for Assistance Agreements That Include Funds Under The American Recovery and Reinvestment Act of 2009, Public Law 111-5, 2 CFR Part 176 (2010).

On September 4, 2009, the city received a $4,875,000 loan from the Indiana Finance Authority (IFA), under the Indiana Wastewater State Revolving Loan Fund Program, to upgrade the city's wastewater treatment plant. The loan included principal forgiveness of $1,769,000 in Recovery Act funds. The city used these funds to rehabilitate and improve its wastewater treatment plant.

Scope and Methodology

Due to the time-critical nature of Recovery Act requirements, we did not perform this assignment in accordance with generally accepted government auditing standards. Specifically, we did not perform certain steps that would allow us to obtain information to assess the city's internal controls and any previously reported audit concerns. As a result, we do not express an opinion on the adequacy of the city's internal controls or compliance with all federal, state, or local requirements.

We made a site visit on September 29, 2010. On May 16, 2011, we visited the city to perform additional work related to Buy American compliance. During our visits, we:

1. Toured the project
2. Visually inspected equipment and materials on site
3. Interviewed IFA and city officials, and their employees

4. Reviewed manufacturers' substantial transformation documentation and other documentation to support compliance with Buy American requirements under Section 1605 of the Recovery Act

Results of Site Visit

The city could not demonstrate that all manufactured goods used on the project met the Buy American requirements set out in Section 1605 of the Recovery Act. Unless the city can comply with Buy American requirements or EPA exercises a regulatory option, the city's project to rehabilitate its wastewater treatment plant is not eligible for $1,769,000 of Recovery Act funds authorized by the state.

In our draft report, we noted 7 of 32 instances where the city could not show compliance with Buy American requirements. In response, the city provided additional documentation and replaced two items to support compliance. We changed our position for six of the seven items after analyzing the additional document and verifying the replacement of the two items. We agreed the six items now comply with the Buy American requirements. For the remaining item—a Kaeser positive displacement blower—no additional information was provided to support that it was manufactured in the United States.

The federal grant to capitalize Indiana's revolving loan fund with Recovery Act funds requires that all projects use manufactured goods produced in the United States, unless certain exceptions apply as provided for in 2 CFR §176.60. The state included the Buy American requirements in the loan agreement with Nappanee.

Section 1605 of the Recovery Act prohibits the use of Recovery Act funds for a project unless all of the iron, steel, and manufactured goods used in the project are produced in the United States. This regulation requires that this prohibition be consistent with U.S. obligations under international agreements, and provides for a waiver under three circumstances: (1) iron, steel, or relevant manufactured goods are not produced in the United States in sufficient and reasonably available quantities and of a satisfactory quality; (2) inclusion of iron, steel, or manufactured goods produced in the United States would increase the overall project costs by more than 25 percent; or (3) applying the domestic preference would be inconsistent with public interest.

Title 2 CFR §176.140 (a)(1) defines a manufactured good as a good brought to the construction site for incorporation that has been processed into a specific form and shape or combined with raw materials to create a material that has different properties than the properties of the individual raw materials. There is no requirement with regard to the origin of components in manufactured goods, as long as the manufacture of the goods occurs in the United States.[1]

There are three substantial transformation questions listed in EPA's guidance document.[2] Affirmative answers to the questions alone are insufficient to support substantial transformation. Documentation is needed to provide a level of specificity and detail for all relevant facts used by the manufacturer to support a claim of substantial transformation, including the manufacturing location and the manufacturing processes for the specific product and/or model number being incorporated into the project. Further, design, planning, procurement, or component production—steps prior to the process of physically working on or bringing together the components of the item incorporated into the project— cannot be considered as constituting or contributing to substantial transformation.

Regarding the seventh item of concern, we noted 11 Kaeser positive displacement blowers that were labeled "Made in Germany." Initially, Kaeser Compressors, Inc., provided a one-page letter claiming their equipment met the Recovery Act requirements. The Kaeser letter claims the company is able to comply with Recovery Act funding requirements "based on using assembly procedures in the United States as directed by the OMB (Office of Management and Budget) in their May, 2009 ruling." Our research did not locate the May 2009 ruling as referred to in Kaeser's letter.

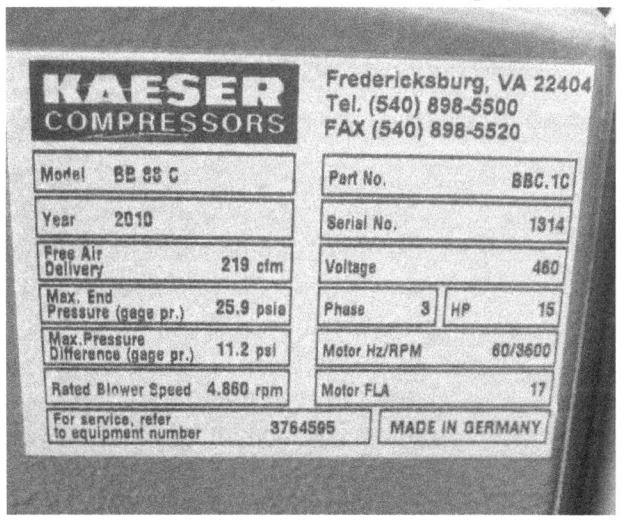

Kaeser blower label, indicating product was made in Germany. (EPA OIG photo)

As a result of a subsequent site visit, the city provided documentation from Kaeser Compressors, Inc., dated October 29, 2010, to support substantial transformation. The letter stated that for Recovery Act-funded projects, Kaeser Compressors, Inc., purchases a base chassis of proprietarily designed components from the parent company, Kaeser Kompressoren, GmbH, located in Germany. The letter further stated that the chassis consisted of components such as the blower block, silencer base, and enclosure. The items added domestically included the electric motor, pulleys, belts, relief valves, and expansion joints. The letter described the building process as mounting and aligning the motor and v-belt pulley drive, adjusting and installing the pressure relief valve(s), and assembling and installing of check

---

[1] Title 2 CFR §176.70(a)(2)(ii).
[2] See *Determining Whether "Substantial Transformation" of Components Into a "Manufactured Good" Has Occurred in the U.S.: Analysis, Roles, and Responsibilities*, dated October 22, 2009.

valves, fan motors, gauges, and switches. Depending on the size and complexity of the specification, additional wiring and setting of ancillary devices may be required. Each unit requires 16 to 20 hours to build. The assembly procedures, combined with the U.S.–sourced items, account for 35 to 50 percent of the package's total value.

Kaeser blowers. (EPA OIG photo)

As previously noted, 2 CFR § 176.140 defines a manufactured good as a good that has been processed into a different form and shape, or combined with other raw materials to create a material that has different properties than the properties of the individual raw materials. Further, 2 CFR § 176.70 states the manufacturing of such goods must occur in the United States.

The October 29 letter does not provide a meaningful and specific technical description of the processes in the United States that would enable us to determine whether the displacement blowers were manufactured in the United States. The letter does not explain how the addition of the drive system (motor, pulley, and belts) changed the properties of the blower chassis manufactured in Germany and imported into the United States, as required by the regulations. Product literature and physical inspection of the equipment at the construction site showed that the chassis manufactured in Germany was essentially a blower without a drive system. The supporting documentation mentioned labor processes and efforts in general, but did not explain how this information relates to changing the properties of the imported blower chassis. The documentation also referred to planning, designing, sourcing, fabricating, building techniques, and testing completed in the United States. EPA guidance, "Determining Substantial Transformation," states that design, planning, procurement, component production, or any other step prior to the process of physically working on or bringing together the components of the item incorporated into the project cannot constitute or be part of the manufacturing process. In addition, the letter does not specifically address the assembly of the blowers incorporated into the Nappanee project. Without additional documentation, there is no evidence to support that the properties of the 11 positive displacement blowers used in the Nappanee project were different from the properties of the blower chassis imported from Germany, as required by 2 CFR § 176.140.

Recommendation

We recommend that the Regional Administrator, Region 5:

1. Employ the procedures set out in 2 CFR §176.130 to ensure compliance with Buy American requirements. In the event that the region makes a determination to retain foreign manufactured goods in the Nappanee project under 2 CFR § 176.130(c)(3), the region should either "reduce the amount of the award by the cost of the steel, iron, or manufactured goods that are used in the project... or take enforcement or termination action in accordance with the agency's grants management regulations."

2. Require the Indiana Finance Authority to verify the City of Nappanee's corrective actions and ensure that replaced items meet the Buy American requirements.

City, Region 5, and State Responses

The Office of Inspector General (OIG) received written comments on the draft report from the City of Nappanee and IFA. The City of Nappanee also provided supplemental documentation to support its comments. Region 5 provided verbal comments during an October 18, 2011, briefing.

The city disagreed with our conclusion that the documentation for several items did not support compliance with Buy American requirements. However, the city has taken action to replace two items with Buy American-compliant components. The city stated that the three guidance documents cited in the report as aids in determination of substantial transformation were not available at the time the city bid the project, and the piecemeal guidance issued by the Agency after the bidding and awarding of the construction project created an inopportune environment in which obtaining comprehensive documentation from manufacturers was very difficult and time intensive. The city also acknowledged Section 1605 of the Recovery Act was in place at the time the project was bid, but practical examples were not available to assist in determining the adequacy of manufacturer documentation. The full text of the city's comments and the OIG's detailed response are included in appendix A.

IFA disagreed with our conclusion that several items did not support Buy American compliance, and noted the city's action to provide additional documentation to demonstrate compliance for five items and the replacement of two products with Buy American compliant products. IFA believes the city's action should demonstrate the city's compliance. The full text of IFA's comments and the OIG's detailed response are included in appendix B.

The Agency provided verbal comments to our draft report during a meeting on October 18, 2011. The Agency disagrees with our position on the Kaeser positive displacement blower. The Agency agreed follow-up action would be necessary to ensure the city's replaced items met the Buy American requirements. On December 22, 2011, representatives from Region 5 and IFA made a visit to the project and verified that two items were replaced. Regarding the remaining four items, the Agency believes the city has provided sufficient documentation to assure compliance with the Buy American requirements.

OIG Comment

Our original recommendation remains unchanged and a second recommendation has been added to address the city's action plan to replace two items. We modified our report based on the additional Buy American documentation provided, and the corrective actions taken by the city to support compliance with the Buy American requirements.

We evaluated the additional documentation provided and verified the corrective actions taken by the city and agreed six of the seven items that had been identified in the draft report comply with the Buy American requirement. For four items, the city provided additional documentation to support compliance with the Buy American requirements, and based on our review of the information we now agree that the four items comply with the requirements. The city replaced two items to meet the Buy American requirements. The removal of these items made $22,198 of Recovery Act funds available for other Recovery Act purposes. Region 5 verified the replaced items on December 22, 2011. We reviewed supporting documentation provided by Region 5 and agree with the actions taken by the city and the region to ensure compliance with the Buy American requirements.

We disagree with the city, IFA, and Region 5 that the Kaeser positive displacement blowers comply with Buy American requirements. The supporting documentation provided for the Kaeser blower is not sufficient to support Buy American compliance. Specifically, it does not provide a meaningful and specific technical description of the processes in the United States that would enable us to determine whether the displacement blowers were manufactured in the United States.

Region 5 stated that EPA Office of Water staff engineers provided "anticipatory" oversight to address the issue of substantial transformation to determine whether the products were actually manufactured in the United States. Office of Water staff engineers opined that substantial transformation is occurring at Kaeser's Fredericksburg, Virginia, facility and that the products are therefore made in the United States. An Office of Water e-mail message to Kaeser, dated November 1, 2010, documents this opinion. During our review, we discussed the November 1, 2010, e-mail with Office of Water staff. EPA's Buy American Q&A Part 2 states,

"Substantial transformation determinations are made by assistance recipients . . . EPA does not and will not make determinations as to substantial transformations . . . EPA's role under §1605 is to review waiver requests. . . ." Office of Water staff providing an opinion on substantial transformation to Kaeser is inconsistent with EPA's guidance and its role under Section 1605 of the Recovery Act.

Status of Recommendations and Potential Monetary Benefits

		RECOMMENDATIONS				POTENTIAL MONETARY BENEFITS (in $000s)	
Rec. No.	Page No.	Subject	Status[1]	Action Official	Planned Completion Date	Claimed Amount	Agreed-To Amount
1	5	Employ the procedures set out in 2 CFR §176.130 to ensure compliance with Buy American requirements. In the event that the region makes a determination to retain foreign manufactured goods in the Nappanee project under 2 CFR § 176.130(c)(3), the region should either "reduce the amount of the award by the cost of the steel, iron, or manufactured goods that are used in the project... or take enforcement or termination action in accordance with the agency's grants management regulations."	U	Regional Administrator, Region 5		$1,769	
2	5	Require the Indiana Finance Authority to verify the City of Nappanee's corrective actions and ensure that replaced items meet the Buy American requirements.	C	Regional Administrator, Region 5			

[1] O = recommendation is open with agreed-to corrective actions pending
   C = recommendation is closed with all agreed-to actions completed
   U = recommendation is unresolved with resolution efforts in progress

City of Nappanee Response to Draft Report and OIG Evaluation

Office of
MAYOR
Larry L. Thompson
Email: nappcity@yahoo.com

City of Nappanee

300 West Lincoln Street
P.O. Box 29
Nappanee, IN 46550-0029

Office Phone: (574) 773-2112
Home Phone: (574) 773-4196
Fax: (574) 773-5878

September 15, 2011

Mr. Robert Adachi
Director of Forensic Audits
United States Environmental Protection Agency
Office of Inspector General
1200 Pennsylvania Avenue, N.W. (2410T)
Washington DC 20460

RE: Draft Site Visit Report
American Recovery and Reinvestment Act Site Visit
of the Wastewater Treatment Plant Improvements Project,
City of Nappanee, Indiana
Project No. OA-FY11-0036

Dear Mr. Adachi,

This correspondence is intended to address the preliminary findings of the U.S. Environmental Protection Agency, Office of Inspector General Draft Site Visit Report: American Recovery and Reinvestment Act Site Visit of the Wastewater Treatment Plant Improvements Project, City of Nappanee, Indiana (Draft Report). Within the aforementioned document, the U.S. Environmental Protection Agency Office of Inspector General (OIG) claim that seven (7) products utilized in the City of Nappanee Wastewater Treatment Plant Improvements Project lack sufficient documentation to meet the American Recovery and Reinvestment Act (ARRA) Section 1605 Buy American requirements and do not meet the criteria outlined in EPA guidance for determining substantial transformation of goods and equipment.

The City of Nappanee believes that five (5) of the seven (7) items now have satisfactory documentation to demonstrate compliance with Buy American via substantial transformation. One (1) of the final two (2) remaining items was replaced with a Buy

American compliant component on September 13, 2011 and the replacement of the remaining item with a Buy American compliant product will occur on or before October 5, 2011.

Table 1: OIG ARRA Buy American Deficiency Summary provides a summary of the items that, according to OIG, did not include the necessary detail and or documentation to demonstrate compliance with Section 1605 of the Recovery Act.

Table 1: OIG ARRA Buy American Deficiency Summary

Section	Item	Manufacturer	Vendor
A	Positive Displacement Blowers	Kaeser	BL Anderson
B	Mag Flow Meters	Siemens	BL Anderson
C	Square D Panels	Schneider Electric	All Phase Electric Supply Co.
D	Peristaltic and Hose Pumps	Watson-Marlow	BL Anderson
E	Check and Gate Valves	Kennedy (M & H) Valve Company	BL Anderson
F	Gate, Globe, Check, Ball, Butterball, and Slo-closed Valves	Milwaukee Valve	Wayne Pipe Supply Company
G	Backflow Preventer	WATTS	Wayne Pipe Supply Company

Specifically, the Draft Report claims that "the documentation provided by the City did not meet the documentation standards for meeting Recovery Act Section 1605 Buy American requirements nor EPA guidance issued for determining substantial transformation of goods and equipment for all project equipment."

Further, the Draft Report states that reasons for the insufficiency rating of the seven remaining items are as follows:

1. Insufficient or no description of the manufacturing processes;
2. No disclosure of the manufacturing site;
3. No transformation questionnaire or alternative documentation to support substantial transformation in the United States; and
4. No documentation or explanation to support answers provided on the substantial transformation matrix.

The Draft Report references three "key" guidance documents to aid in the determination of substantial transformation of goods utilized in the project, which is classified by OIG as the primary deficiency for the remaining seven (7) items. It is important to note that these guidance documents were not available at the time the City of Nappanee Wastewater Treatment Plant Improvements Project was bid. The delayed and piecemealed guidance issued by EPA after the bidding and awarding of the construction contract(s) for the Nappanee Wastewater Treatment Plant project created an inopportune environment in which obtaining comprehensive documentation from manufacturers was very difficult and time intensive. The City of Nappanee acknowledges that Section 1605 of the Recovery Act was in place at the time the project was bid, but practical examples were not available at this time and resulted in uncertainties in determining the adequacy of manufacturer documentation. However, in spite of these obstacles, the City, its consulting engineer (Commonwealth Engineers, Inc.), its contractor (R.E. Crosby), and several equipment representatives and manufactures continue to make every effort to adhere to the guidance that was developed and distributed after the project was bid. The City has proceeded with due diligence in acquiring the documentation throughout the project and after its completion.

> **OIG Response 1:** We recognize that the Recovery Act's Buy American requirements were new, and projects were required to be under contract or construction 12 months after the Recovery Act was signed. The city accepted funds from Indiana through the Wastewater State Revolving Loan Fund Program. The loan agreement between the city and IFA requires the city to comply with all federal requirements applicable to the loan when funded by the Recovery Act. Further, paragraph (r) on page 18 of the loan agreement's standard conditions requires Buy American compliance. If the city was unclear about the procedures necessary to fulfill its responsibilities under the loan agreement, the city should have sought guidance from the state. In addition, EPA published several training and guidance documents on its public Internet site to assist recipients in meeting Recovery Act requirements.

In addition to the untimely issuance of the final Buy American documentation guidance as outlined above, it appears as though documentation provided to OIG staff by Commonwealth Engineers, Inc. on behalf of the City of Nappanee, was not acknowledged or considered in the preparation of the Draft Report. In particular, additional substantial transformation documentation was provided by Milwaukee Valve, Kaeser, and Square D and transmitted to OIG staff via e-mail in May 2011 and June 2011 but it does not appear that this additional documentation was reviewed or addressed in the Draft Report. It was also the understanding of the City of Nappanee and those working on behalf of the City that secondary documentation, namely shipping manifests and bills of lading, would be considered to determine the actual origin of substantial transformation or assembly, but it does not appear any of this information was reviewed or considered by OIG in the Draft Report.

Despite the issues outlined above, each item listed in **Table 1: OIG ARRA Buy American Deficiency Summary** is individually addressed in the remaining portions of this correspondence whereby the findings, factual accuracy of OIG's findings, and concurrence or non-concurrence of the City of Nappanee are stated and summarized. In addition, a discussion on existing and recent substantial transformation documentation is also included along with a discussion on the shipping information provided, where applicable.

A.   Kaeser Positive Displacement Blowers

1. OIG Comment: "Made in Germany" labels were found on the equipment.

    Nappanee Response: The City does not refute the presence of these labels on the chassis and blower blocks of the positive displacement blowers. However, the documentation mentioned below should serve to prove that the blowers meet Buy American provisions.

2. OIG Comment: The Letter dated June 16, 2009 to Mr. Mark Gasvoda of BL Anderson references a May 2009 United States Office of Management and Budget (OMB) ruling from May 2009 that validated the blowers meet the ARRA funding requirement. The OIG was unable to locate said ruling.

    Nappanee Response: Given OIG's lack of acknowledgement of the May 2009 ruling, statements regarding this ruling are hereby retracted from this review. The May 2009 ruling is not needed to prove compliance with Buy American provisions.

    OIG Comment: The letter dated October 29, 2010 from Kaeser to the City of Nappanee was provided to support substantial transformation. The letter states that for ARRA funded projects that Kaeser, Compressors, Inc. purchases a base chassis (blower block, silencer base, and enclosure) of proprietarily designed components from the parent company Kaeser Kompressoren, GmbH located in Germany. The electric motor, pulleys, belts, relief valves, and expansion joints were added domestically. Product Literature and inspection indicates that the chassis manufactured in Germany is essentially a blower without a drive system. The documentation provided did not explain how the addition of the drive system substantially changed or transformed the character and use of the good manufactured in Germany and imported to the U.S.

    Nappanee Response: Kaeser Compressors, Inc. provided additional correspondence to the City of Nappanee dated May 18, 2011, which further elaborates on the substantial transformation of the positive displacement blowers at the Fredericksburg Virginia manufacturing site. This correspondence further describes the time, cost, skill level of employees, and substantial value added to the final product to be utilized specifically for wastewater applications such as the City of Nappanee Wastewater Treatment Plant Improvements Project. We request that OIG further consider the May 18, 2011 correspondence for the determination that substantial transformation occurred in the United States. In addition, Kaeser Compressors, Inc. has retained the services of Foley & Lardner LLP to assist in responding to questions raised by OIG in the Draft Report. As outlined in the letter dated September 14, 2011 from Foley & Lardner LLP to Mayor Larry Thompson, a comprehensive response is expected to be provided to OIG by September 21, 2011[3]. Please be advised that the aforementioned letters can be reviewed in further detail in **Attachment A**.

---

[3] The OIG received and reviewed the cited response. No additional evidence was provided which would change our position.

3. <u>OIG Comment</u>: Documentation mentioned labor processes and efforts in general but did not provide the specific labor and cost detail utilized to substantially transform the equipment.

    <u>Nappanee Response:</u> The May 18, 2011(**Attachment A**) letter signed by Stephen Horne of Kaeser Compressors Inc. clearly indicated on page three that "The assembly procedures combined with the domestically sourced items account for 35 to 50 percent of the packages total value." Per the response above, additional details on the substantial transformation process in the U.S. will be forthcoming by September 21, 2011.

4. <u>OIG Comment</u>: Planning, designing, sourcing, fabricating, building techniques and testing were all stated to be completed in the United States; however, EPA guidance states that these tasks do not constitute substantial transformation.

    <u>Nappanee Response:</u> Regardless of EPA opinion that "planning, designing, sourcing, fabricating, building techniques and testing" do not constitute substantial transformation, the May 18, 2011 documentation provided by Kaeser Compressors, Inc. (**Attachment A**) clearly states that the <u>actual building</u> of the blower occurs in the U.S. at the facility located at 511 Sigma Drive Fredericksburg, Virginia. The term "building" in this context is synonymous with the term substantial transformation. Please be advised that the forthcoming September 14, 2011 will contain further detail on the activities performed to substantially transform the blowers in the U.S. as questioned by OIG in the Draft Report.

In the opinion of the City of Nappanee, it appears that OIG did not thoroughly review the information provided by BL Anderson and Kaeser Compressors, Inc. Of particular interest is the Order Confirmation dated January 12, 2010 which consists of four pages and includes the following relevant information that further demonstrates substantial transformation in the U.S.:

- Number of items in the order to be shipped to Nappanee;
- Model number of positive displacement blowers;
- ARRA notation for the blowers which indicates substantial transformation occurred in the United States;
- Method of delivery;
- Origin of delivery;
- Projected delivery date; and
- Specific language stating "assembly at Fredericksburg."

In addition, a key element to the documentation provided by Kaeser Compressors, Inc. was not acknowledged by OIG, which is the e-mail provided by Kaeser Compressors, Inc. in which Kristen Kroner of USEPA Drinking Water State Revolving Fund Team Office of Groundwater and Drinking Water states that: "Based on the additional information provided, we believe substantial transformation is occurring in the U.S. at your Fredericksburg facility." This e-mail correspondence was sent to Stephan Dagovitz, the District Manager of Kaeser Compressors,

Inc. on November 1, 2010 and was provided to OIG staff on May 20, 2011. The aforementioned correspondence has been attached in **Attachment A** for review.

> **OIG Response 2:** We reviewed Kaeser Compressors, Inc.'s, letter dated October 29, 2010, to EPA's Office of Water. The letter contained the same information as the May 18, 2011, Kaeser letter referred to in the city's response. We found the information in the letter to be insufficient to enable us to determine whether the displacement blowers were manufactured in the United States, as noted in this report's "Results of Site Visit" section. We received and reviewed the Foley & Lardner, LLP, report and found no new information to support the items being manufactured in the United States.
>
> We were aware of the e-mail sent by an employee from EPA's Office of Water. We find no authority in Section 1605 of the Recovery Act or the relevant regulations at 2 CFR Part 176, "Requirements for Implementing Sections 1512, 1605, and 1606 of the American Recovery and Reinvestment Act of 2009 for Financial Assistance Awards," that would authorize EPA to make a determination of substantial transformation. In fact, EPA's Determining Substantial Transformation clearly states that "EPA does not and will not make determinations as to substantial transformation or the U.S. or foreign origin of manufactured goods." Since Kaeser Compressors, Inc., is an affiliate of Kaeser Kompressoren, GmbH, and "the base chassis of proprietary designed components" was obtained from the parent, we need to clearly understand the precise steps and costs completed in the United States versus the process and steps completed in Germany for the actual blowers used in the Nappanee project.

B.   Siemens Mag Flow Meters

1. OIG Comment: Dutch labels were found on the equipment.

    Nappanee Response: The City acknowledges the Dutch labels on the cable of the Siemens Mag Meter and these cables were replaced on September 13, 2011.

2. OIG Comment: Documentation provided stated that the meters "undergo final assembly, testing, user-defined programming and labeling in the Siemens Configuration Center located in Spring House, PA USA." This document was deemed to be insufficient for the determination of substantial transformation in the United States.

    Nappanee Response: BL Anderson Company, the Siemens Flow Meter Product Line Representative, replaced the Dutch-produced flow transmitter, cabling, and remote wall mount kit with Buy American compliant equipment on September 13, 2011. Substantial transformation documentation for this equipment has been included for review in **Attachment B**.

OIG Response 3: We acknowledge the city's action taken to have BL Anderson Company, the Siemens Flow Meter Product Line Representative, replace the Dutch-produced flow transmitter, cabling, and remote wall mount kit with Buy American compliant equipment. Based on the stated action taken, we added a report recommendation to the Agency to verify that the item has been replaced with Buy American–compliant equipment. On December 22, 2011, the Region 5 and IFA staff visited the project and verified the city's replacement of the Siemens Flow Meter. We reviewed supporting documentation provided by Region 5 to support their visit and the city's compliance with the Buy American requirements. We agreed that the action taken by the city and the region have resolved the question of compliance. We modified our report accordingly.

C. Square D Electrical Panels

1. OIG Comment: No label of origin found on the panels.

    Nappanee Response: The City of Nappanee acknowledges that no labels were found on the panels; however, Brady Dryer of Commonwealth Engineers, Inc. did provide documentation to OIG on June 3, 2011 verifying that the Square D panels were substantially transformed in Peru, Indiana.

2. OIG Comment: Insufficient Buy American documentation was provided.

    Nappanee Response: Again, the City of Nappanee questions the review of documentation provided to OIG staff. On June 3, 2011 an e-mail was sent by Brady Dryer of Commonwealth Engineers, Inc. to John Flynn and Jean Bloom which included documentation describing relevant characteristics of the Peru, Indiana Square D manufacturing facility. This documentation was neither acknowledged by OIG staff via e-mail nor was it referenced in the OIG Draft Report. Nonetheless, Square D has provided additional documentation in the form of the Substantial Transformation Examination Checklist which includes the required narrative and has been attached for review in **Attachment C**. This documentation should provide adequate evidence that the panels, including circuit breakers, were substantially transformed in Peru, Indiana.

OIG Response 4: We reviewed the information contained in the June 3, 2011, e-mail and found it insufficient to support compliance with Buy American requirements. We acknowledge that not all of the information provided and reviewed was referenced in our draft report. A substantial transformation matrix was provided with insufficient explanation of the manufacturing process.

We reviewed the additional information provided by Commonwealth Engineers, and determined that sufficient documentation has been provided to support compliance with the Buy American requirements. We revised the final report accordingly.

D. Watson-Marlow Peristaltic Pump

1. <u>OIG Comment:</u> Buy American documentation not sufficient.

> <u>Nappanee Response:</u> Further review and discussion with Watson-Marlow have indicated that the peristaltic pumps do not meet ARRA Buy American requirements. A letter stating this misunderstanding and the inability of this item to meet Recovery Act Section 1605 Buy American provisions was provided by BL Anderson, the manufacturer's representative, on May 25, 2011 to the City of Nappanee. In particular, this letter discusses Watson-Marlow's improper application of the North American Free Trade Agreement (NAFTA) in the context of compliance with Recovery Act Section 1605. The above-mentioned correspondence can be reviewed in greater detail in **Attachment D**. As the City had relied on Watson-Marlow's assertion that the pumps complied with Buy American until the misapplication of NAFTA came to light, this delay created difficulties for Nappanee in order to utilize available avenues to comply with Buy American without creating undue delays in the completion of the project.

> However, the City will comply with the required Buy American compliance requirements of ARRA by replacing the Watson-Marlow peristaltic pumps with the Pulsafeeder, Inc. Chem-Tech Series XPV peristaltic pump, which are substantially transformed in Punta Gorda, FL. Additional documentation has been provided in **Attachment D** for review. Of particular interest is a letter dated February 17, 2010 signed by Jefferey Bye, the Director of Marketing and Business Development which states that the Chem-Tech Series SPO products may include components from the United States, Canada, South Korea, Taiwan, and China, but are substantially transformed in Punta Gorda, FL.

> Additional information has been requested regarding the specific steps in the manufacturing process, labor required, skill level of employees, the addition of substantial value, and percentage of foreign versus domestic components in the Chem-Tech Series peristaltic pumps and the documentation will be sent to OIG upon receipt. This equipment will be installed to replace the Watson-Marlow perastaltic pumps at the Nappanee WWTP within the next three (3) weeks per correspondence provided by Mark Gasvoda of BL Anderson on September 14, 2011 (**Attachment D**).

OIG Response 5: We acknowledge the city's planned action to replace the noncompliant Watson-Marlow peristaltic pump and added a report recommendation to the Agency to verify the item replacement with a Buy American–compliant pump. On December 22, 2011, Region 5 and IFA staff visited the project and verified the city's replacement of the pump. We reviewed supporting documentation provided by Region 5 and determined the actions taken by the city and the region have resolved the question of compliance. We modified our report accordingly.

E. Kennedy (M & H) Valve Company Check and Gate Valves

Kennedy Valve, Clow Valve, and M&H Valve are subsidiary companies of the McWane Company. Each company manufactures various kinds of valves, and the logo for each company appears on each valve. BL Anderson, the supplier of the Check and Gate Valves, determined that Kennedy Valve provided the items installed at the Nappanee WWTP project. The Kennedy check and gate valves are substantially transformed in Elmira, New York. Representatives of Kennedy Valve provided a Substantial Transformation Examination checklist and related supporting narratives on September 2, 2011, which has been included in **Attachment E**. This information states that all components, except for $15 worth of foreign items are substantially transformed in the United States at the Elmira, New York facility.

1. OIG Comment: Insufficient or no description of the manufacturing processes.
      Nappanee Response: Page 3 September 2, 2011 Substantial Transformation Examination Checklist (**Attachment E**) describes the manufacturing process.

2. OIG Comment: No disclosure of the manufacturing site.

   Nappanee Response: The September 2, 2011 Substantial Transformation Examination Checklist (**Attachment E**) clearly states that the valves for the Nappanee Wastewater Treatment Plant Improvements Project were substantially transformed in Elmira, New York.

3. OIG Comment: No transformation questionnaire or alternative documentation to support substantial transformation in the United States; and

   Nappanee Response: The Substantial Transformation Examination Checklist was completed on September 2, 2011 and has been included in **Attachment E** review.

4. OIG Comment: No documentation or explanation to support answers provided on the substantial transformation matrix.
      Nappanee Response: The Substantial Transformation Examination provided on September 2, 2011 includes narratives as required per the Draft Report and has been included in **Attachment E** for review.

The above documentation should serve to prove that the Kennedy Valves meet the ARRA Buy American requirements as they were substantially transformed in Elmira, New York.

OIG Response 6: We reviewed the additional information included in the city's response and determined that sufficient documentation has been provided to support compliance with the Buy American requirements. We revised the final report accordingly.

F. Milwaukee Valve Gate, Globe, Ball, Butterball, and Slo-closed Valves

Milwaukee Valve provided documentation regarding ARRA Buy American compliance on May 26, 2011 to Brady Dryer of Commonwealth Engineers, Inc. This correspondence was e-mailed to John Flynn of EPA on May 26, 2011 by Brady Dryer. No acknowledgement of this e-mail message and supporting correspondence was received and it appears this information was not considered for the Draft Report.

Per the Draft Report, additional documentation was requested from Milwaukee Valve. Thomas LaGuardia of Milwaukee Valve responded to this request in correspondence dated September 6, 2011 in the form of a completed Substantial Transformation Examination Checklist with narratives. The general deficiencies noted in the EPA audit are addressed below and the noted correspondence has been included in **Attachment F**.

1. OIG Comment: Insufficient or no description of the manufacturing processes;

   Nappanee Response: See page 2 and 3 of the September 6, 2011 Substantial Transformation Examination Checklist describing the manufacturing process, which has been included in **Attachment F**.

2. OIG Comment: No disclosure of the manufacturing site;

   Nappanee Response: Correspondence from Milwaukee Valve, dated May 26, 2011 and September 6, 2011 include a statement indicating the Prairie du Sac Wisconsin facility is the manufacturing sites of the valves provided for the Nappanee Wastewater Treatment Plant Improvements Project. This correspondence has been included in **Attachment F** for review.

3. OIG Comment: No transformation questionnaire or alternative documentation to support substantial transformation in the United States was available; and

   Nappanee Response: The Substantial Transformation Examination Checklist was completed on September 6, 2011 and has been included in **Attachment F** for review.

4. OIG Comment: No documentation or explanation to support answers provided on the substantial transformation matrix.

   Nappanee Response: The Substantial Transformation Examination checklist includes narratives required per the Draft Report and has been included in **Attachment F** for review.

The above documentation should serve to prove that the Milwaukee Valve does meet the ARRA Buy American requirements.

OIG Response 7: We acknowledge that not all of the information provided and reviewed was referenced in the draft report. We reviewed the information contained in the May 26, 2011, e-mail and found it insufficient to support compliance with Buy American requirements. The information did not disclose the manufacturing location. We reviewed information provided with the city's response to the draft report, and determined that sufficient documentation has been provided to support compliance with the Buy American requirements. We revised the final report accordingly.

G. WATTS Backflow Preventer
General statements of ARRA Buy American Compliance were provided by WATTS to the City of Nappanee in correspondence dated February 11, 2010. This correspondence did not include substantial transformation information, which recently has been provided by Ames Fire & Waterworks, a subsidiary of WATTS, on September 6, 2011. General information regarding substantial transformation of the Backflow Preventer, including a factory tour of the Ames facility, has been included for review in **Attachment G**.

The general deficiencies noted in the Draft Report are addressed below and the noted correspondence and relevant information are attached.

1. OIG Comment: Insufficient or no description of the manufacturing processes;

    Nappanee Response: Page 1 of the September 6, 2011 correspondence from Ames Fire & Waterworks generally describes the manufacturing process. The Substantial Transformation Examination Checklist with detailed narratives has been requested and will be submitted to OIG upon receipt; however, general substantial transformation discussion and a factory tour of the Ames Fire & Waterworks facility in Woodland, California are included in **Attachment G**.

2. OIG Comment: No disclosure of the manufacturing site;

    Nappanee Response: The September 6, 2011 correspondence from Ames Fire & Waterworks states that the components of the backflow preventer in question are manufactured in Woodland, California whereby approximately 75% to 80% of the raw material is domestically provided.

3. OIG Comment: No transformation questionnaire or alternative documentation to support substantial transformation in the United States; and

    Nappanee Response: The Substantial Transformation Examination Checklist and corresponding narratives have been requested and will be submitted to OIG upon receipt; however, a general substantial transformation discussion and a factory tour of the Ames Fire & Waterworks facility in Woodland, California are included in **Attachment G**.

4. OIG Comment: No documentation or explanation to support answers provided on the substantial transformation matrix.

    Nappanee Response: The Substantial Transformation Examination Checklist and corresponding narratives have been requested and will be submitted to OIG upon receipt; however, a general substantial transformation discussion and a factory tour of the Ames Fire & Waterworks facility in Woodland, California are included in **Attachment G**.

This documentation should serve to prove that the WATTS Backflow Preventer does meet the ARRA Buy American requirements; however, as indicated above, additional documentation will be provided to OIG upon receipt.

OIG Response 8: We reviewed the information provided in response to the draft report, and determined sufficient documentation has been provided to support compliance with the Buy American requirements. We revised the final report accordingly.

Conclusion

The City of Nappanee has diligently worked to demonstrate compliance with Buy American requirements. Based upon the recent submissions from manufacturers and/or suppliers, it is the City of Nappanee's position that five (5) of the seven (7) deficient items noted in the Office of Inspector General Site Visit Draft Report dated August 16, 2011 now meet the ARRA Buy American requirements. The City has provided detailed documentation for these five manufacturers which should satisfactorily demonstrate Buy American compliance through substantial transformation.

To address the remaining two items, the City believes that the Siemens Mag Flow Meters are now in compliance with Buy American provisions, as the non-compliant components have been replaced with components which were substantially transformed in Springhouse, Pennsylvania. Documentation from Siemens describing the substantial transformation process has been provided in **Attachment B**. The remaining item, the Watson-Marlow Perilstalic Pumps, will be replaced with Pulsafeeder, Inc. Chem-Tech Series XPV peristaltic pumps by October 5, 2011. The Pulsafeeder pumps are substantially transformed in Punta Gorda, FL as stated in **Attachment D** and additional detail provided by Pulsafeeder will be submitted to OIG for review upon receipt.

We appreciate the opportunity to respond to the Office of Inspector General Draft Site Visit Draft Report for the Nappanee Wastewater Treatment Plant Improvements Project. We sincerely hope that this correspondence and the attachments will suffice in addressing the findings in the referenced Draft Report. If you should have any further questions or concerns, please contact Brady Dryer at Commonwealth Engineers, Inc. via e-mail at bdryer@contactcei.com or by phone at (317) 888-1177.

Sincerely,

Mayor Larry Thompson
City of Nappanee

Attachments
Attachment A: Kaeser Documentation
Attachment B: Siemens Documentation
Attachment C: Square D Documentation
Attachment D: Watson-Marlow and Pulsafeeder Documentation
Attachment E: Kennedy Valve (M&H) Documentation
Attachment F: Milwaukee Valve Documentation
Attachment G: WATTS Documentation

cc: Steve Marquardt, Chief, Section 2, State and Tribal Programs Branch, Region 5 (sent via email)
Laura Cossa, State Program Lead, State and Tribal Programs Branch, Region 5 (sent via email)
Gale Gerber, Utilities Manager, City of Nappanee, Indiana (sent via email)
Al Stong, Project Manager, Commonwealth Engineers, Inc. (sent via email)
Jim McGoff, Director of Environmental Programs, Indiana Finance Authority (sent via email)
Mark Downey, President, Commonwealth Engineers, Inc. (sent via email)
Al Stong, Project Manager, Commonwealth Engineers, Inc. (sent via email)
Brady Dryer, Compliance Manager, Commonwealth Engineers, Inc. (sent via email)

Indiana Finance Authority Response to Draft Report and OIG Evaluation

September 15, 2011

VIA FIRST CLASS MAIL   **Copies sent via email to: John Trefry (trefry.john@epa.gov)**
                                              Jean Bloom (bloom.jean@epa.gov)

Robert Adachi
Director of Forensic Audits
United States Environmental Protection Agency
Office of Inspector General
1200 Pennsylvania Avenue, N.W. (2410T)
Washington, DC 20460

Re: Draft Site Visit Report
        American Recovery and Reinvestment Act Site Visit of
        Wastewater Treatment Plant Improvements Project,
        City of Nappanee, Indiana
        Project No. OA-FY11-0036

Dear Mr. Adachi:

The Indiana Finance Authority (IFA) is in receipt of the U.S. Environmental Protection Agency (EPA) - Office of Inspector General's (OIG) "Draft" Site Visit Report dated August 16, 2011 (Draft Report) regarding the above referenced matter. As required by the Draft Report, the IFA hereby submits its written response to the findings and recommendations of the Draft Report.

Introduction

The IFA believes the Draft Report inaccurately concludes the IFA "did not comply with documentation standards for meeting Recovery Act Section 1605 Buy American requirements nor EPA guidance for determining substantial transformation of goods and equipment." This IFA response to the Draft Report demonstrates that IFA has complied with its responsibilities regarding the Buy American requirements set forth in the American Recovery and Reinvestment Act of 2009 (ARRA) and in subsequent Buy American Guidance documents issued by EPA.

The IFA requests that references to the "IFA", located on page two (2) and page six (6) of the Draft Report be removed from the final OIG Site Visit Report as the inclusion of IFA as a non-compliant party is factually inaccurate. Pursuant to EPA issued Guidance Document (EPA-816-F-10-062) dated August 2010, the State's role (as performed by the IFA) and responsibility during the implementation of ARRA was to provide "oversight and check project compliance". As the below response demonstrates, the IFA developed a comprehensive compliance program for Buy American compliance which included significant oversight measures and project inspections for not only the City of Nappanee (City or City of Nappanee) but for all projects funded with ARRA dollars. As is documented below, the IFA not only met its responsibility as mandated by ARRA and EPA, but initiated measures that exceeded EPA's requirements to better assure that recipients of ARRA funds and the manufacturers of equipment supplied to ARRA funded projects adhered to the requirements associated with ARRA funded projects.

Background

IFA executed a Grant Agreement with the EPA to use funds made available by ARRA dated August 20th, 2009. This Grant Agreement provided a total award to the Indiana Clean Water State Revolving Fund (CW SRF) Loan Program of $94,447,500.00. The ARRA required all funds to be under an assistance agreement and begin construction by February 17, 2010. IFA solicited "shovel ready" projects in the State of Indiana and entered into forty-three (43) Financial Assistance Agreements with CW SRF loan participants by January 28, 2010. One of the 43 loan participants was the City of Nappanee. IFA executed a Financial Assistance Agreement with the City of Nappanee on September 4th, 2009 in the amount of $4,875,000.00, this amount included $3,106,000.00 of base SRF funds and $1,769,000.00 of ARRA dollars. It is important to note that the City of Nappanee closed its loan before EPA issued key guidance documents relating to Buy American requirements and substantial transformation.

Despite the untimely issuance of pertinent guidance documents pertaining to Buy American, particularly the documentation required to demonstrate substantial transformation, the IFA worked diligently with Nappanee and all of its loan participants to ensure that each loan participant was aware of any federal guidance and requirements. IFA strongly believes that it fulfilled its role and responsibility relating to Buy American compliance and further believes that each of its loan participants, including the City of Nappanee, made every attempt to comply and has complied with issued Buy American guidance.

Response

I. IFA has fulfilled its roles and responsibilities set forth in EPA issued Buy American compliance guidance documents. IFA has developed and implemented a comprehensive Buy American compliance program, which includes oversight inspection procedures for all ARRA funded projects.

Pursuant to EPA guidance dated August 2010 which outlines the roles and responsibilities of the State, IFA developed and implemented compliance oversight measures of ARRA funded projects at the pre-construction, construction, and post-construction phases. IFA dedicated substantial time, resources, and personnel to assist its SRF borrowers, the party ultimately responsible for the project's compliance, to meet ARRA obligations and maintain adequate documentation, to decide how and when to properly apply de minimis and substantial transformation decisions.

At the pre-construction phase, every SRF borrower which received ARRA funds certified to IFA that all ARRA project requirements would be followed. Further, the engineering consultant retained by the SRF borrower responsible for drafting the design and bid specifications for the ARRA funded project(s) certified to IFA that bids were prepared in accordance with ARRA Buy American regulations. This certification included required Buy American contract provisions which IFA instructed engineering consultants to include in every procurement contract associated with all ARRA funded projects. At contract award, IFA required that all contractors and sub-contractors certify that every procurement contract associated with an ARRA funded project contain the required Buy American contract provisions and follow Buy American procurement and documentation requirements. Representatives from IFA attended pre-construction meetings to answer questions and provide guidance to ARRA project stakeholders. Finally, IFA reviewed manufacturer documentation used to demonstrate Buy American compliance and provided suggestions to improve documentation in order to comply with evolving EPA guidance.

During the construction phase, IFA set a goal of inspecting every ARRA funded project at construction milestones of 25%, 50%, 75% and 100% completion. IFA created an ARRA Inspection Checklist to supplement its existing inspection checklist to capture ARRA-specific requirements. Further, IFA requested that each ARRA borrower provide all manufacturer submissions to IFA for anticipatory review. IFA reviewed submissions from manufacturers, as those documents were provided to IFA from the ARRA borrower or its engineering consultant in order to provide oversight and suggested follow-up action. IFA relayed changes in Buy American documentation guidance to ARRA borrowers via email updates and newsletter articles. IFA engineers and compliance personnel regularly met with ARRA project stakeholders to clarify documentation requirements.

At the post-construction phase, IFA requested that ARRA borrowers complete and return the EPA State ARRA Inspection Checklist to IFA for review prior to the release of final payments. At this time, IFA provided final comments on the sufficiency of Buy American documentation submitted by manufacturers and suggested follow-up steps. IFA also reviewed de minimis waiver items to ensure compliance with the requirements of utilizing the waiver.

The above mentioned compliance steps were taken with the City of Nappanee. At the pre-construction phase, the City of Nappanee provided the certification required by IFA stating that the project would follow all ARRA project requirements. The City of Nappanee's engineering consultant provided a certification that bids were prepared in accordance with Buy American regulations and that the required Buy American contract provisions would be included in each and every procurement contract. In addition, the contractors and sub-contractors involved in the Nappanee project certified that the required Buy American contract provisions would be included in each procurement contract. IFA staff attended meetings with the City of Nappanee and its consulting engineer and provided information on the Buy American requirements and provided an opportunity to answer questions. IFA staff reviewed manufacturer documentation provided by Nappanee and if needed, provided suggestions to improve documentation in order to comply with the evolving EPA guidance. During the construction phase, IFA staff inspected the Nappanee project on multiple occasions in order to verify construction progress, SRF program compliance, and ARRA compliance. The Nappanee project was inspected on the following dates:

- March 11, 2010 (15% completion)
- May 7, 2010 (30% completion)
- October 7, 2010 (80% completion)
- March 16, 2011 (100% completion)
- May 4, 2011 (100% completion)
- May 16, 2011 (100% completion)

Through the development and implementation of the aforementioned comprehensive compliance program, IFA strongly believes it not only met its obligation outlined in EPA guidance to "oversee and check project compliance" of ARRA funded projects but it went above and beyond its obligation to help ensure that its SRF borrowers understood and complied with all the ARRA requirements, including the Buy American requirements that have proven to be complicated and were issued well after many communities closed their ARRA loan, including the City of Nappanee. IFA believes that the inclusion of IFA as a non-compliant party in regard to not meeting its Buy American requirements is factually inaccurate and respectfully requests that the references made to "IFA" in the Draft Report should be removed from any final OIG Site Visit Report associated with the City of Nappanee's project. See supporting State Revolving Fund Compliance documentation in Attachment A.

II. The City of Nappanee has taken significant corrective action and has made every attempt to obtain additional documentation to support its compliance with the Buy American requirements.

Project Background

The Nappanee Wastewater Treatment Plant (WWTP) Improvements project will produce water quality and environmental benefits by correcting a deficiency in aerobic sludge treatment and sludge storage capacity at the WWTP, as well as replacing an inefficient blower system, and converting the disinfection process from chlorine gas to ultra-violet disinfection to eliminate a potential safety hazard. The project went to bid on June 8, 2009 and received SRF financing on September 4, 2009. The notice to proceed with construction was issued just ten days after loan closing, on September 14, 2009 so as to meet the "shovel-ready" requirements of ARRA.

The City of Nappanee met its due diligence requirement by working with its consultant engineer to obtain documentation from manufacturers and suppliers to demonstrate compliance with the Buy American requirements of ARRA. Untimely and evolving EPA guidance related to documentation requirements created challenges for the City that they have worked diligently to address by contacting manufacturers, suppliers, and vendors and engaging in a very time-intensive discussion with these parties in order to obtain primary and secondary Buy American documentation. Following OIG's site visit in May 2011, the City has taken substantial steps to correct the seven (7) identified deficiencies. As indicated in Table One, the City has taken further action by: (a) providing updated substantial transformation documentation for five (5) of the seven (7) items; and by (b) replacing two (2) non-compliant products with Buy American compliant products. The above action should demonstrate that the City has complied with its Buy American requirements.

Table One: OIG Preliminary Findings and Action Taken

Item	Manufacturer	Vendor	Action	IFA Concur/Do Not Concur
Positive Displacement Blowers	Kaeser	BL Anderson	Updated substantial transformation documentation provided	Do Not Concur
Mag Flow Meters	Siemens	BL Anderson	Non-compliant item replaced with Buy American compliant item on 9/13/11	Do Not Concur (Product in compliance as of 9/13/11)
Square D Panels	Schneider Electric	All Phase Electric Supply Co.	Updated substantial transformation documentation provided	Do Not Concur
Peristaltic and Hose Pumps	Watson-Marlow	BL Anderson	Non-compliant item to be replaced with Buy American compliant item	Do Not Concur (Product will be in compliance no later than 10/05/11)
Check and Gate Valves	Kennedy (M & H) Valve Company	BL Anderson	Updated substantial transformation documentation provided	Do Not Concur
Gate, Globe, Check, Ball, Butterball, and Slo-closed Valves	Milwaukee Valve	Wayne Pipe Supply Company	Updated substantial transformation documentation provided	Do Not Concur
Backflow Preventer	WATTS	Wayne Pipe Supply Company	Updated substantial transformation documentation provided	Do Not Concur

Listed below are the seven (7) items identified in Table One with further explanation of the steps the City has taken to comply with Buy American requirements.

Kaeser Positive Displacement Blowers

A May 18, 2011 letter provided by Kaeser Compressors, Inc. to the City of Nappanee clearly describes the substantial transformation process conducted in the Fredericksburg, Virginia facility. This letter contains the specific labor and cost detail which was missing as of OIG's site visit to the City in May 2011. Kaeser describes the substantial transformation process as requiring 16-20 hours of build time and that the Positive Displacement Blowers contain 35-50 percent of domestically sourced items. Kaeser's substantial transformation process was confirmed as sufficient for Buy American compliance purposes by Kirsten Kroner from the Drinking Water SRF Team Office at EPA Headquarters in Washington, D.C. in an email to Stephan Dagovitz of Kaeser dated November 1st, 2010. IFA concurs with

EPA's analysis, and concludes that the Kaeser Positive Displacement Blowers comply with Buy American requirements. See supporting Kaeser documentation in <u>Attachment B.</u>

> **OIG Response 9:** See the "Results of Site Visit" and appendix A of this report for OIG comments on Kaeser Positive Displacement Blowers.

Siemens Mag Flow Meters

A September 2, 2011 letter provided by BL Anderson, supplier of the Siemens Mag Flow Meter indicates that the magnetic flowmeter transmitter, standard cabling, and remote wall mount kit supplied to the City of Nappanee were manufactured in Denmark. The transmitter, cabling, and wall mount kit are components which function together by providing flow information to the flow meter itself. These items are provided by Siemens as a set. As of September 13th, 2011, BL Anderson has removed the non-compliant transmitter, cabling, and wall mount kit and replaced them with a transmitter, cabling, and wall mount kit substantially transformed in Springhouse, Pennsylvania. The transmitter is substantially transformed from components, including circuit boards and enclosures. Additional documentation describing the substantial transformation process is forthcoming. As such, IFA believes that the Siemens Mag Flow Meters are in compliance with Buy American requirements. See currently available Siemens documentation in <u>Attachment C.</u>

> **OIG Response 10:** See appendix A for OIG comments on Siemens Mag Flow Meters.

Square D Electrical Panels

Square D provided substantial transformation documentation to the City of Nappanee dated August 30, 2011 which adds additional detail to a June 3rd, 2011 letter previously provided to OIG by Commonwealth Engineering. Both documents describe the manufacturing and transformation process at the Square D facility in Peru, Indiana. Square D employs 500 people at their Peru facility where the Electrical Panels are transformed in a process that takes 4.5 hours. The Electrical Panels contain approximately 75% domestic materials. IFA does not concur with OIG's preliminary finding that Square D's documentation is insufficient, and believes that substantial transformation of the Electrical Panels occurred in Peru, Indiana. Therefore, IFA believes the Electrical Panels meet the Buy American requirements. See supporting Square D documentation in <u>Attachment D.</u>

> **OIG Response 11:** See appendix A for OIG comments on Square D Electric Panels.

Watson-Marlow Peristaltic Pump

Initially, the City relied on the assertions of Watson-Marlow in a letter dated April 23, 2009 that the pumps it supplied to the City complied with Buy American requirements because they fell under the North America Free Trade Agreement (NAFTA); however, the City received a letter from the supplier of the Watson-Marlow Pumps, BL Anderson, on May 25, 2011 stating that the NAFTA exemption was misapplied and the Watson-Marlow Pumps (Pumps) did not comply with Buy American, as the Pumps are manufactured in the United Kingdom. Per a September 14, 2011 email from BL Anderson, the non-compliant Pumps will be replaced with Buy American compliant Pulsafeeder pumps no later than October 5, 2011. The new pumps have been substantially transformed in a process involving inspection, machining, assembly, programming, testing, and packaging in Punta Gorda, Florida at the Pulsafeeder manufacturing facility. See currently available supporting Watson-Marlow documentation in <u>Attachment E.</u> Additional documentation describing the substantial transformation process is forthcoming.

OIG Response 12: See appendix A for OIG comments on Watson-Marlow Peristaltic Pump.

Kennedy Valve (M&H) Company Check and Gate Valves

Kennedy Valve, M&H Valve, and Clow Valve are subsidiary companies of the McWane Company, and each company manufactures several kinds of valves which bear the company logo and name of each subsidiary. Documentation provided by Kennedy Valve, the manufacturer of the Check and Gate Valves, to the City of Nappanee on September 2, 2011 describes the substantial transformation process the Valves undergo at the Kennedy Valve manufacturing facility in Elmira, New York. The Check and Gate Valves contain only $15 worth of non-domestic components, and are transformed through a complex process involving melting iron, machining castings, and assembling the final product. IFA does not concur with OIG's preliminary finding and believes that the Kennedy Valve transformation process is sufficiently time, labor, and cost intensive to meet EPA standards, and that the Check and Gate Valves comply with Buy American requirements. IFA believes that the Kennedy Valve documentation supports the City's assertion that Valves have been substantially transformed in Elmira, New York. See supporting M & H Valve documentation in <u>Attachment F.</u>

OIG Response 13: See appendix A for OIG comments on Kennedy Valve (M&H) Company check and Gate Valves.

Milwaukee Valve Gate, Globe, Ball, Butterball, and Slo-closed Valves

Documentation provided to the City of Nappanee by Milwaukee Valve on September 6, 2011 provides sufficient detail to determine that substantial transformation of Milwaukee Valve Gate, Globe, Ball, Butterball, and Slo-closed Valves occurred at the Prairie du Sac, Wisconsin manufacturing facility. 95% of the Milwaukee Valve Gate, Glob, Ball, and Butterball, and Slo-closed Valves are domestically sourced, and the substantial transformation process takes approximately eight (8) hours. IFA does not concur with OIG's preliminary finding that documentation for the item is deficient, and believes that the Milwaukee Valve Gate, Globe, Ball, Butterball, and Slo-closed Valves comply with Buy American requirements. See supporting Milwaukee Valve documentation in Attachment G.

> **OIG Response 14:** See appendix A for OIG comments on Milwaukee Value Gate, Glove, Ball, Butterball, and Slo-closed Valves.

Watts Backflow Preventer

Documentation provided to the City of Nappanee by Watts on September 8, 2011 provides sufficient detail to determine that substantial transformation of the WATTS Backflow Preventer occurred in the manufacturing facility of a Watts' subsidiary, Ames Fire & Waterworks, in Woodland, California. The Backflow Preventer contains 75%-80% domestic materials and the substantial transformation process requires multiple complex processes to fabricate and manufacture the product using highly skilled laborers. Therefore, IFA does not concur with OIG's preliminary finding and believes that Watts has complied with Buy American requirements. See supporting Watts documentation in Attachment H.

> **OIG Response 15:** See appendix A for OIG comments on Watts Backflow Preventer.

Conclusion

The IFA has met its obligation under ARRA to provide compliance oversight to the City of Nappanee, Indiana by requiring signed ARRA certifications from the City, its consultant engineer, and its contractor. These certifications describe all ARRA-related requirements in detail, including Buy American and require that the certifying party acknowledge and adhere to these requirements throughout the project. IFA further verified compliance by reviewing manufacturer documentation, and providing suggestions to the City to improve documentation in adherence to evolving EPA Buy American guidance.

IFA visited the Nappanee Wastewater Treatment Plant Improvements Project several times throughout construction, and after the project was complete. Because these efforts are above and beyond IFA's requirement to "provide oversight and check project compliance," any reference to IFA as a non-compliant party is factually inaccurate. IFA respectfully requests that references to "IFA" as a non-compliant party are removed from the final OIG Site Visit Report.

OIG Response 16: We acknowledge IFA's compliance program, outlined in the above response, to meet EPA's guidance to "oversee and check project compliance" of Recovery Act–funded projects and the challenges encountered with the Buy American requirements. The purpose of our review was to determine whether the City of Nappanee complied with selected requirements of the Recovery Act. We did not perform a detailed review of IFA's roles and responsibilities or work performed to assure compliance on the Nappanee project. We modified our final report based on IFA's comments to the draft report and removed the reference to IFA as a noncompliant party.

In addition, IFA believes that the City of Nappanee has worked diligently to comply with its obligation regarding the Buy American requirements. The City has provided updated manufacturer documentation proving that substantial transformation has occurred in the United States for five (5) of the seven (7) deficient items identified by OIG in their Draft Report. The non-compliant components of the Siemens Mag Flow Meters have been replaced and the non-compliant Watson-Marlow Pumps will be replaced with Buy American compliant products thereby satisfying Buy American requirements. IFA believes that the City will be found to have met its Buy American requirements on all deficient items listed in the Draft Report.

Thank you for the opportunity to respond to the Draft Report. If you have any questions, please contact me at 317-234-2916.

Sincerely,

James P. McGoff
Director of Environmental Programs
Indiana Finance Authority

Attachments

Attachment A: State Revolving Fund Compliance Documentation

Attachment B: Kaeser Documentation

Attachment C: Siemens Documentation

Attachment D: Square D Documentation

Attachment E: Watson-Marlow Documentation

Attachment F: Kennedy (M&H) Valve Documentation

Attachment G: Milwaukee Valve Documentation

Attachment H: WATTS Documentation

cc: Steve Marquardt, Chief, Section 2, State and Tribal Programs Branch, Region 5 (sent via email)

        Laura Cossa, State Program Lead, State and Tribal Programs Branch, Region 5 (sent via email)

        Honorable Larry Thompson, Mayor, City of Nappanee, Indiana (sent via email)

        Gale Gerber, Utilities Manager, City of Nappanee, Indiana (sent via email)

        Al Stong, Project Manager, Commonwealth Engineers, Inc. (sent via email)

        Brady Dryer, Compliance Manager, Commonwealth Engineers, Inc. (sent via email)

        Kendra W. York, Public Finance Director, Indiana Finance Authority

        Deborah Wright, General Counsel, State Revolving Fund Loan Program, Indiana Finance Authority

Distribution

Office of the Administrator
Regional Administrator Region 5
Assistant Administrator for Water
Agency Follow-Up Official (the CFO)
Agency Follow-Up Coordinator
General Counsel
Associate Administrator for Congressional and Intergovernmental Relations
Associate Administrator for External Affairs and Environmental Education
Director, Grants and Interagency Agreements Management Division,
    Office of Administration and Resources Management
Audit Follow-Up Coordinator, Region 5
Public Affairs Officer, Region 5
Director, Water Division, Region 5
Chief, State and Tribal Programs Branch, Region 5
Public Finance Director, Indiana Finance Authority, Indiana
Mayor, City of Nappanee, Indiana
Superintendent/Manager, Waste Water Utilities, City of Nappanee, Indiana

www.ingramcontent.com/pod-product-compliance
Lightning Source LLC
Chambersburg PA
CBHW081801280526

45789CB00008B/2955